# Contents

# Introduction

The Wheel of the Year symbolizes the passing seasons and holidays marked by practicing pagans of many stripes and lovers of nature alike. Our household is influenced by several flavors of paganism, and I started writing this book as a reference for our home and how we interpret and celebrate the seasons. The celebrations and rituals described here represent an affirmation of our values and our human need for ritual and celebration.

There are many ways to celebrate the seasons and the way we do this is rooted in home, nature, and simple practices like cooking that connect us to the cycles of the year, the cycles of life, and our own personal histories. They are meaningful and ground us but don't in fact need to be religious at all. These are things that are common to all of us, in our own ways, and this book is a record of our household's way.

sometimes wonder how others celebrate the seasons, so I decided to make this book available to anyone who might also be interested in such things.

The recipes within this book come from many sources and have evolved over the years into my own. First, of course, my mother's recipes are a foundation of my approach to cooking in general and several of the recipes herein, including my childhood favorites - homemade drop biscuits and gravy, zucchini quiche, and gingerbread cake. The accidentally high proportion of vegetarian recipes can also be attributed to my upbringing - as a child of parents influenced by the back-to-the-land movement of the 60s and 70s. Finally, we make our home in the San Francisco Bay area and the ingredients used in my recipes are often multicultural and seasonal to the area, reflecting our connection to this very special place in the world for food.

I hope you enjoy this book and I hope it inspires you to think about what traditions connect you to your family, communities, and the natural world during your own celebrations and observances.

# Notes

# Candlemas/Imbolc

We always celebrate Imbolc, also known as Brighid's day, on February 1 as a time for clearing out winter's cobwebs. It is an awakening, a way to snap out of the cabin fever that can set in while the light is short.

We observe Candlemas the night before on January 31, gathering as many candles as possible and using them to light up the whole living room. I take the sheets, towels, and winter coats outside and hang them on the line overnight (unless it's raining) so Brighid will come in the night and bless them.

In the morning we spend the day at home, cooking with the color white and freshening the house. Dungeness, a cold water crab, and kumquats are seasonal, special treats here in California. Open the windows and let the crisp air blow through and clear away stagnancy.

Homemade drop biscuits with gravy

Leek and potato soup

Dungeness crab fried rice

Kumquat pound cake

Ritual: Divination

Ritual: Protective Embroidery

# Homemade drop biscuits and gravy

serves 4

## things you need

**Biscuits**

3/4 cup milk

1 tsp apple cider vinegar

1.5 cups all purpose flour

2 tsp baking powder

1/4 tsp salt

1/4 cup butter

**Gravy**

6 Tbsp butter

1/4 cup thinly sliced roast beef, chopped

1/4 cup flour

2 cups milk

1/4 tsp dried thyme

Salt and pepper

1  Prepare biscuits. Combine flour, baking powder, and salt.

2  Add butter to flour mixture in small slivers and work into large crumbs with fingers.

3  Add vinegar to milk to make instant buttermilk and drizzle into crumbed mixture, mixing with a fork until moistened.

4  Flour hands and knead dough in a bowl about 10 times until just holding together. Work in a little more flour if it is sticking to your fingers.

5  Roll into balls, flatten slightly, and place on greased pan about an inch apart. Bake at 425F for about 15 minutes.

6  While biscuits are baking, prepare gravy. Melt butter in a pan and add rosemary and beef, cut into small slivers.

7  Slowly add flour, stirring constantly with a spoon while scraping the bottom of the pan.

8  Slowly add milk and combine to prevent lumps. Cook on low, stirring frequently, until thickened to desired consistency.

9  Season to taste and serve gravy over biscuits and top with a fried egg.

# Leek and potato soup

serves lots

vegetarian

things you need

3 leeks, cleaned and chopped

4 medium potatoes, peeled
and cubed

2 carrots, peeled and sliced

2 T. butter

Salt and pepper

Heavy cream

Water or broth

1  Sautee leeks in butter until wilted.

2  Add potatoes, carrots, and water or broth to just cover.

3  Simmer on low 20-30 minutes until vegetables are tender.

4  Use a stick blender to carefully puree.

5  Season with salt and pepper and add more water or broth if needed for desired consistency.

6  Divide into bowls and then add a splash of cream to serve.

Waiting to add the cream when served allows for longer storage of leftover soup.

# Dungeness crab fried rice

serves 4

things you need

2 cups rice, prepared and
refrigerated in advance

2 Tbsp vegetable oil

1/2 yellow onion, diced

1/4 cup carrot, diced

1/4 cup celery, diced

2 tsp sugar

salt

1 tsp soy sauce

1/2 tsp garlic powder

1 egg, beaten

1 cup dungeness crab

1 Heat oil in a pan and add onion, carrot, and celery. Sautee until softened slightly.

2 Mix in rice, sugar, garlic powder and soy sauce.

3 Cook for 5 minutes, stirring occasionally. Add salt to taste.

4 Make a well in the middle of the rice mixture. Add more oil if needed and add egg. Scramble egg in center until cooked and then mix into rice.

5 Add crab meat (you can substitute shrimp if you can't find crab) and mix in.

# Kumquat pound cake

serves many

vegetarian

things you need

2 sticks unsalted butter, room temperature

3 cups sugar

1 cup sour cream

3 cups flour

1/2 tsp baking soda

1 tsp vanilla

1/2 Tbsp grated kumquat

6 eggs

1  Preheat oven to 325F

2  Cream butter and sugar. Add sour cream, eggs, and grated kumquat and blend until smooth.

3  Sift four and baking soda into wet mixture and combine gradually.

4  Grease and flour a bundt pan. Pour batter into pan and bake 1 hour 20 minutes until done.

# Ritual: Divination

Spread cold ashes from a fire across the hearth and leave them overnight. In the morning, examine them for a sign that Brighid visited.

## Things you need

Cold ashes from a fire burned on Candlemas.
A brick, stone, or iron hearth or simply a brick, a flat stone, or a cast iron pan.

If you see no sign of Brighid's visit in the morning ashes, pour a cupful of milk on the ground outside as an offering.

If the weather is bad on Imbolc day, expect a short winter. If the weather is good, expect a long one.

# Ritual: Protective Embroidery

Protective embroidery is not about sewing well. It is about the energy you put in to thinking about your loved one while sewing.

## Things you need

Handkerchief or Bandana

Embroidery needle

Thread, Embroidery floss, or dental floss

I like to choose a corner of a handkerchief and just start sewing stitches without a plan. I stay within a 1/2 inch square space and make the pattern that comes to me, whether it is someone's initial or a symbol or pattern. This is a good place for a beginner to start, but of course there are many ways to practice protective embroidery.

# Notes

Mill by MSG David Largent (CC BY 2.0)

# Spring Equinox

Where we live, the Equilux—when the hours of day and night are equal— is a few days before the Equinox itself, and I like to celebrate this moment of balance in the year, when light meets darkness, during the Equilux. The date is different depending on where you are. Even though it is not the commonly accepted time for the pagan holiday, the feeling of that tipping point is important to me because in March of every year I feel a bit like I'm going over the edge of a cliff after the long winter.

We take every opportunity to celebrate Spring. It is an invigorating and hopeful time, full of new energy. We will observe the Equilux, the Equinox, Easter, the nearest full moon and new moon; whatever chance we get we will celebrate it! Spring is not a time to be beholden to rules or dogma and we are not above a chocolate rabbit or marshmallow chicken in a basket!

Quick pickled carrots, daikon, and jalapeños

Prosciutto bánh mì

Lemony mint couscous with chickpeas

Sour cream honey almond cake

Ritual: Natural food dyes

Ritual: Combining Traditions

# Quick pickled carrots, daikon, and jalapeño

serves many

vegan

## things you need

Carrots, cut in sticks

Daikon, cut in sticks

2 jalapeños, quartered with seeds removed

Coarse salt

Sugar

White vinegar

Water

Place carrots, daikon, and jalapeños in a pasta strainer and coat lightly with salt. This will draw some of the water out of the vegetables,. Leave in the sink to drain for about 15 minutes. Then squeeze extra liquid from the vegetables.

2  Stuff vegetables into a clean jar. Add about a Tablespoon of surar.

3  Fill jar halfway with white vinegar and fill the rest of the way with water.

4  Close and seal the jar and refrigerate at least overnight up to 1 month.

5  Serve as a garnish for bahn mi and use the jalapeños to make a delicious salsa. Also makes a great condiment for hot dogs!

# Pancetta bánh mì

serves 6

## things you need

6 slices prosciutto

Pickled carrots, daikon, and japaleños

Fresh cilantro

Fresh thai basil

Fresh mint leaves

Mayonnaise

6 crusty French baguettes

1 Cut the rolls long ways, but don't cut all the way through. They should sit open like hot dog buns.

2 Spread a very thin layer of mayonnaise over the bread.

3 Place one thin slice of prosciutto in the center of the split roll.

4 Stuff the roll with pickled vegetables and fresh herbs.

5 Wrap tightly in cling film and pack for a picnic!

# Lemony mint couscous

serves many

vegan

things you need

1 1/2 cup couscous

1/2 tsp salt

2 1/2 cups boiling water

Juice and zest of 2 lemons

1/4 cup olive oil

1 can chickpeas, drained

Large handful of chopped mint

1/2 cup chopped parsley

1/2 cup chopped green onions

1/2 cup black olives, diced finely

1 small cucumber, diced

1 In a large bowl, add salt, lemon zest, and boiling water to couscous. Cover and let sit for 5-10 minutes. Then uncover and fluff lightly with a fork.

2 Add vegetables, herbs, and chickpeas to couscous.

3 Combine olive oil and lemon juice and whisk to mix, then pour over couscous mixture.

4 Gently combine all ingredients but don't overmix or it will become sticky.

5 Eat immediately or refrigerate before eating. If you wait overnight the herbs will infuse fully into the couscous.

# Sour cream honey cake

Serves 16

vegetarian

things you need

1 cup sliced almonds

1 1/4 cups whole wheat flour

3/4 cup all purpose flour

1/2 tsp baking soda

1/2 tsp salt

3/4 cup butter at room

Temperature

1 cup honey

4 eggs

1/4 cup sour cream

1 Preheat oven to 325F. Lightly grease a 9 inch round cake pan. Sprinkle 3/4 of the sliced almonds into the bottom of the pan and spread out evenly.

2 Combine flour, baking soda, and salt and set aside.

3 In large bowl, mix together butter, honey, and eggs. Gradually  mix in the flour mixture until smooth. Then stir in sour cream and the remaining 1/4 cup sliced almonds.

4 Pour batter over almonds in pan and bake 50 to 55 minutes until the cake starts to separate from the sides of the pan.

5 Remove from oven and cool for about 15 minutes before removing cake from pan, almond side up, and cooling completely. Dust with powdered sugar and serve.

Mellifluous by David Goehring (CC BY 2.0)

# Ritual: Food dyes

Natural food dyes to use
if part of your Spring
Equinox celebration
includes dying eggs.

## things you need

Vinegar

Water

Salt

Baking soda

Beet juice

Turmeric

Water from boiled red

Cabbage, reduced

Pink: 1cup beet juice, 1 Tbsp
vinegar, 1/2 tsp salt

Yellow: 1 Tbsp turmeric, 1 cup
water, 1 Tbsp vinegar, 1/2 tsp
salt

Blue: 1 cup red cabbage water
reduction, baking
soda added in pinches until
blue

# Combining Traditions

It sounds strange to call combining traditions a part of our spiritual practice, but I can think of nothing more honest. And I can think of nothing more spiritual than honesty.

## things you need

Your personal history

Your personal beliefs

An open mind

# Notes

Freezing Fire by Emilio Küffer (CC BY-SA 2.0)

# Walpurgisnacht/ Beltane

The climax of all of the celebrations of Spring is the celebrations of Walpurgisnacht and Beltane on April 30 and May 1. April 30 is also my husband's birthday so he gets to choose the menu. Below are his thoughts on the holiday.

"Walpurgisnacht is a night to awaken the demons of winter that have slumbered for too long and to indulge hedonistic desires. Named after St. Walpurgis, who was a nun killed for witchcraft, it is a connection to Samhain as those are the two times of the year when the veil between the living and the immaterium is thinnest. It is the oldest continued holiday of the western pagan tradition, very important in druidic rites and would include fires from the burning of herbs or peat. It is a celebration of the darker half of the year. The last chance to dance with the devil, so to speak."

Following Walpurgisnacht is Beltane, a time for planting seeds of all kinds and burning protective fires. That makes it a great day for gathering for a bbq. Beltane is also the first day of the year for fairies to take over from the darker spirits. Sometimes we will build bird or fairy houses, sometimes we will plant flowers. We often see tiny hummingbird nests in our yard, made out of spider webs. These nests built for new life out of another creature's hunting snares are the perfect representation of this transitional holiday.

Zucchini quiche

Saffron vegetable soup

Crème fraiche chicken

German chocolate cake

Ritual: Wishes fire starters

# Zucchini quiche

serves 6

vegetarian

## things you need

1 small zucchini, diced

1/2 yellow onion, diced

9 inch, deep frozen pie crust

3/4 cup Gruyere (swiss) cheese, cubed

1/4 cup shredded cheddar cheese

3 eggs, lightly beaten

1/2 cup half and half

1/2 cup cream

1 pat butter

2 T. minced parsley

Salt and pepper

1/4 tsp ground nutmeg

1  Preheat oven to 375F

2  Sautee onion and zucchini in butter until soft

3  Evenly distribute Gruyere and vegetables on frozen pie crust

4  In a bowl, whisk eggs, cream, milk, and spices. Pour mixture over cheese and vegetables

5  Place filled pie crust on baking sheet, cover the outer ring of crust with aluminum foil and bake for 30 minutes. Remove foil after 30 minutes, then sprinkle cheddar cheese on top of the quiche and bake for an additional 15 minutes or until firm.

# Summer vegetable soup

Serves lots

vegan

## things you need

2 Tbsp olive oil

1 yellow onions, chopped

8 medium red potatoes, diced

4 carrots, chopped

2 leeks, washed and chopped

2 cups string beans, ends
removed

3 quarts water or vegetable
stock

handful of dry spaghetti,
broken in pieces

1/4 cup pesto

1 tsp. saffron

Salt and pepper

1  Sautee onions and leeks in olive oil.

2  Add potatoes, carrots, and  water or stock.

3  Add saffron, salt, and pepper and simmer for 30 minutes.

4  Add beans, pesto, and spaghetti and simmer 10-15 more minutes.

5  Season again with salt and pepper to taste.

# Crème fraiche chicken

Serves 4

things you need

1 cup crème fraiche

1/4 cup Dijon mustard

1 Tbsp fresh thyme

1 tsp salt

2 large garlic cloves, diced

3 lbs. skinless chicken thighs

1. In a large bowl, combine crème fraiche, mustard, thyme, garlic, and salt.

2. Add chicken and make sure all pieces are covered .

3. Cover in plastic wrap and  set aside at room  temperature for 2 hours.

4. Preheat oven to 400F

5. Place the marinaded chicken on a rimmed baking sheet and bake for 45 minutes or until cooked through.

# German chocolate cake

Serves 8

vegetarian

## things you need

2 oz. Baker's Sweet
Chocolate, chopped

1 cup all purpose flour

1/3 cup cocoa powder

1/4 tsp. baking soda

1/4 tsp salt

1 stick plus 1 Tbsp. unsalted
butter at room temperature

1 cup sugar

2 eggs + 1 egg yolk

1 tsp. vanilla extract

1/2 cup buttermilk

Mini chocolate chips

For filling

3/4 cup heavy cream

1/2 cup granulated sugar

2 egg yolks

1 1/4 cups unsweetened
coconut flakes, toasted

3/4 cup pecans, toasted
and finely chopped

3 Tbsp unsalted butter cut in
pieces

1/4 tsp. salt

Heat oven to 350F and coat a 13x9 inch baking dish with butter.

Heat the chocolate in a double boiler and stir until completely melted. Remove from heat and set aside.

Combine flour, cocoa powder, baking soda, and salt in a large bowl. For filling, combine cream, sugar, and egg yolks in a saucepan over medium heat, stirring constantly until the mixture thickens and coats a spoon, about 8 minutes.

In a separate bowl, cream the butter and sugar. Add the eggs one at a time and then the egg yolk, beating after each until smooth.

Add the vanilla and melted chocolate and mix until evenly combined.

Add a third of the dry ingredients and mix in completely. Add half the buttermilk. Repeat until all of the dry ingredients and buttermilk are combined.

Pour the batter into the greased pan and bake about 35 minutes. Test with a toothpick. When done, cool on a wire rack for about 1 hour.

Transfer to a medium bowl, add the remaining ingredients, and stir until evenly blended. Let cool at room temperature.

Transfer cake to a cutting board and cut into equal thirds, each about 4x9.

Spread a third of the filling over the top of one layer, add second layer and spread another third of filling on top, finish with the third layer and the final third of the filling. Garnish with mini chocolate chips.

# Ritual: Wishes fire starters

Use these to start your ceremonial fires throughout the year. Burn the wishes in the fire to help make them come true.

## things you need

Egg carton

Candle wax, cut into small chunks

Dryer lint

Dental floss

Strips of paper with your wishes written on them

Cut egg carton to separate the cups. Fill with dryer lint, fold the corners over, and tie closed with dental floss. Leave a 6-8 inch tail of floss after tying. Melt candle wax in a jar over boiling water and dip each bundle into the wax, submerging and coating completely. Allow to dry on a paper towel or newspaper. Finally drip a dime sized amount of melted wax on top of each bundle and stick a wish to each one.

# Notes

# Notes

Ferris wheel by D. Laird (CC BY 2.0)

# Summer Solstice

It is easy to celebrate the sun on the longest day of the year and most of us don't need a traditional holiday to do it. We celebrate the sun with more fire, of course, usually in the form of a BBQ. Seasonal corn and fruit and herbs make summer feel like summer.

Our backyard is overrun with passionflower vines and lemon verbena as well as the culinary herbs we grow in the garden. The neighbors use the lemon verbena to scent their beeswax products and I use the passionflower to make a relaxing tincture to use throughout the rest of the year.

An easy alternative to the tincture, for those who don't want to deal with all that fuss, is simply to combine passionflower leaves with mint leaves and water in a glass jar and let it sit out in the sun to make sun tea. Can there be a better offering to the sun gods?

Blueberry, mango salad with ginger lime dressing

Tappen-churri

Sweet corn soup with bbq shrimp

Peach and mint sangria

Ritual: Passionflower tincture

Ritual: Tea spells

# Blueberry Mango Salad

Serves many

vegan

things you need

4 cups cubed mango

1 cup blueberries

1 lime

1/4 cup water

1/4 cup sugar

1 Tbsp candied ginger

1 Heat water and sugar on the stove until almost boiling.

2 Zest the lime peel in long strips, carefully removing the pith. Add lime peel to heating sugar water.

3 Stir until sugar is dissolved, add the juice of the lime, then immediately remove from heat and set aside.

4 Place cubed mango and blueberries in a large bowl.

5 While dressing is cooling, finely dice candied ginger.

6 Remove lime zest from dressing and pour dressing over fruit. Stir gently to combine.

7 Sprinkle diced candied ginger on top and serve.

# Tappen-churri

Serves many

vegan

things you need

1/4 cup finely diced black olives

Handful of finely cut fresh basil leaves

1/4 cup finely diced cashews

About 1/4 cup olive oil

2 Tbsp chopped capers

2 tsp chopped garlic

Juice of 1/2 to 1 lemon

Handful of finely cut fresh parsley

1 Combine all ingredients in a sealable glass container and mix well.

2 For a marinade, add more olive oil and lemon juice.

3 For a spread, add less olive oil and lemon juice. Serve with fresh bread.

4 Tastes best after sitting overnight. Store refrigerated.

# Sweet corn soup with bbq shrimp

Serves 6-8

things you need

3 cups sweetcorn, including juices

1 full garlic bulb

Salt and pepper

2 large Yukon gold potatoes

3-4 pounds raw shrimp, heads on

1 stick butter

1/2 cup Worcestershire sauce

1/4 cup Old Bay seasoning

Tabasco sauce to taste

2 lemons

Peel the outside of the garlic, cut off the tip and roast in the oven at 435 until soft.

In a large pot, combine corn and juices, cubed potatoes, shrimp heads, and just enough water to cover. Bring to a boil.

Squeeze roasted garlic out of its skin and into the soup pot. Add more water to cover if needed and return to a boil.

Remove from heat, remove shrimp heads and discard. Then, using a stick blender, blend soup until smooth. Salt and pepper to taste. Return to low heat and cover.

Devein the shrimp but leave the shell on.

Coat the bottom of a large roasting pan with olive oil and spread shrimp out, no more than two layers deep.

Top with enough old bay to cover and Worcestershire sauce. Bake at 325 for about 15 minutes.

Top with remaining butter, divided into 1/2 Tbsp pats, remove from oven, and stir to combine

Serve soup in bowls and add shrimp and Tabasco to taste. Serve with crusty French bread.

# Peach and mint sangria

Serves 4

things you need

2 large peaches
1 bottle white wine
3/4 cup peach brandy
1 liter peach seltzer water

In a glass pitcher, lightly muddle peaches with brandy. Add wine and seltzer and mix.

# Passionflower tincture

Passionflower is thought to have a calming effect and grows like crazy once established.

## things you need

Chopped Passionflower leaves, vines, and flower buds

Vodka

Cheesecloth

Dark colored sealable glass container

Cover chopped plant matter in vodka. Cover with a lid and leave in a cool dark place for 2 weeks,  shaking occasionally. Strain through cheesecloth into dark glass container. I add 1-2 droppers full to a small amount of water and drink before bed. Do not give to children.

Zones by Zixii (CC BY-SA 2.0)

# Ritual: Tea spells

Boxed herbal teas are a lazy witch's shortcut to simple tea spells.

## things you need

Love: Rose hip tea
Luck: Mint tea
Happiness: Lemon Balm
Health: Ginger tea
Gratitude:  Blackberry leaf

Depending on the element you wish to summon to assist your spell, combine the tea with water, burn it, plant it, or throw it to the winds!

# Lammas/Lugh's Day

First harvest means baking bread and challah is my favorite bread to bake, taken one step further here by turning it into French toast. First harvest also symbolizes a time when we can finally reap the benefits of all of our work and struggles. This symbolism is why Lammas is traditionally used for handfasting ceremonies. My husband and I were married on Lammas and the hopped cider recipe here is the same one he made for our wedding.

There are as many ways to have a handfasting ceremony as you can imagine, but I included a snippet of ours here. Feel free to borrow it and make it your own.

Challah french toast with blackberry coulis

Rib eye steak with fresh salsa

Puffed cherry pie

Hopped cider

Ritual: Handfasting ceremony

# Challah French toast with blackberry coulis

Serves 8-10

vegetarian

## things you need

1 1/3 cups flour

1 pk active dry yeast

2/3 cup warm water

1/4 cup honey

1/4 cup vegetable oil

3/4 tsp salt

1 egg

1 egg yolk

1 egg white

2 cups whole wheat flour

2 tsp sesame seeds

2 pints blackberries

2 Tbsp. agave syrup

1 cup milk

1 egg, beaten

1 tsp. nutmeg

1 tsp. cinnamon

Combine 1 cup white flour and yeast. Stir together warm water, honey, oil, and salt. Add to flour mixture with egg and egg yolk. Beat with electric mixer on low for 30 seconds and on high for 3 minutes.

Gradually add all whole wheat flour and as much of the remaining white flour as you can.

On a lightly floured surface, knead in enough of the white flour to make a moderately stiff dough. Place in a greased bowl, turn, cover, and let rise until double, about 1 hour.

Punch down dough. Cover and let rest 10 minutes. Divide dough into 3 pieces and roll into ropes.

On a greased baking sheet, braid ropes together and tuck ends under. Cover and let rise in a warm place until almost double, 30-60 minutes.

Mix together the remaining egg white and 1 T. water. Brush over loaf. Sprinkle with sesame seeds.

Bake at 350F 25-30 min or until golden. Cover with foil to prevent overbrowning for last 10 minutes if needed. Cool on rack.

Combine blackberries with agave syrup and blend.

Heat a pan on the stove with vegetable oil. Combine 1 cup milk, egg, nutmeg, and cinnamon in a wide low bowl.

Slice challa. Dip each slice into milk mixture and place in hot oiled pan. After a few minutes, turn over and cook on the other side. Place on plate and serve with blackberry coulis.

# Ribeye steak with fresh salsa

## Serves 4

2 large rib eye steaks

1 Tbsp. vegetable oil

1 Tbsp. butter

Salt and pepper

Garlic powder

4-5 roma tomatoes

Handful fresh cilantro

1 tsp. salt

2 large cloves garlic

1-2 pickled or canned

jalapeños

Chop tomatoes and put them in a blender with garlic cloves, jalapeño, cilantro, and 1 tsp. salt (more or less of anything to taste). Blend until smooth and set aside.

2 Season both sides of steaks with salt, pepper, and garlic powder. Add to a heavy, hot, oiled pan, about 5 minutes per side.

Turn off heat and divide butter. Set stakes aside and melt butter on top.
3 After rested a few minutes serve with the salsa on top. Tastes great with fried eggs.

# Puffed cherry pie

Serves 8

Vegan

things you need

4 cups pitted cherries

1 stick margarine

1 cup flour

1/4 tsp. salt

1 cup sugar

1 cup milk

1 tsp. baking powder

1. Preheat oven to 375F. Melt margarine in baking pan.

2. Heat cherries in separate pan on the stove.

3. Mix dry ingredients in mixing bowl. Add milk and mix. Pour mixture into baking pan.

4. Arrange cherries on top of mixture. Bake 30-40 minutes.

# Hopped cider

Serves many

## things you need

5 gallon carboy

5 gallons pressed apple cider from local farmers market

1 cup champagne yeast

3/4 oz Citra Dried Hop Pellets

# Notes

# Handfasting ceremony

Lugh's day is a time for joining ceremonies. If you are considering marrying someone you love, use this as an opportunity for a traditional one year and one day trial marriage.

Will you share each other's laughter and dreams and honor each other always?

Will you share each other's pain and seek to ease it? Share the burdens of life so that they may be lighter?

Will both of you look for the brightness in life and the positive in each other? Will you dream together to create new realities and hopes? And always remind each other of your love?

# Notes

# Notes

Pleurotus sp. (oyster mushroom) by Daniel Neal (CC BY 2.0)

# Autumn Equinox

Magical, comforting autumn! I don't know anyone who doesn't get a little bit of a pull towards the kitchen, towards home, and towards family in the autumn. Tradition seems to be in the air that we breathe at this time of the year and I am reminded of apple picking and hunting trips.

The day around the equinox when the light changes ever so slightly but always noticeably drives me into the kitchen too. It is all about comfort food and it is a feeling of reassurance that we have the safety of our homes and families as the days become shorter and darker.

In addition to the fun apple carving ritual I describe here, this is also a perfect time for sewing and weaving projects, or leatherworking and even taxidermy. Home projects like painting or repairing create the feeling of security too.

Breakfast hash frittata

Puttanesca sauce with meatballs

Curried red lentils

Vanilla oatmeal cookies

Ritual: Carving apple heads

# Breakfast hash frittata

Serves many

vegetarian

## things you need

1 potato, diced small

1 small yellow onion, diced

1 red bell pepper, diced small

1 Tbsp. olive oil

6 eggs

1/4 cup milk or cream

Salt and pepper

1/4 cup shredded cheese

Preheat oven to 400F.

2 Heat oil in an oven safe skillet. Add potato, onion, and bell pepper and saute until soft.

3 Whisk eggs and milk in a bowl until frothy. Add to skillet and distribute evenly. Season with salt and pepper.

4 Cook over medium low heat until the eggs start to set. Then move to the oven.

5 Cook in oven until puffed up and slightly browned on top. Top with cheese and remove from oven when melted.

6 Allow to cool slightly, then slice and serve.

# Puttanesca sauce with meatballs

Serves 4-6

## things you need

1 28 oz. can crushed Italian tomatoes

1 yellow onion, minced

2 garlic cloves, minced

1/2 cup pitted black olives, chopped

2 Tbsp. capers, drained

1/2 tsp. salt

Pinch of red pepper flakes

3 Tbsp. olive oil

1/2 to 1 cup red wine

1/2 lb. ground lamb

1/2 lb. Italian sausage meat

2 Tbsp. Worcestershire sauce

2 Tbsp. flour

1-2 Tbsp. olive oil

1 Tbsp. fresh basil, chopped

Salt and pepper

2 tsp. garlic salt

1 small yellow beet, minced

2 garlic cloves minced

To make sauce, heat olive oil in a saucepan, add onion, and cook until soft. Add olives, capers, salt, garlic, and red pepper flakes and sautee 1 minute.

Add tomatoes and simmer until reduced slightly, about 20 minutes. Taste and add more salt if needed. If too acidic, add a teaspoon of sugar.

While the sauce is cooking, add all other ingredients to a large bowl and mix with fingers to combine.

Form meat mix into small balls, about 1 inch across.

Heat another 1-2 Tbsp. olive oil in a cast iron pan and cook meatballs, turning to brown  evenly and cook through.

Remove meatballs from pan and stir into sauce. Deglaze the meatball pan with wine, scrape up the bits of caramelized meat, and pour the wine into the sauce. Stir to combine and simmer for 5 more minutes.

Serve with bread, pasta, or spaghetti squash.

# Curried red lentils

Serves 6-8

vegan

## things you need

2 Tbsp. olive oil

1 yellow onion, chopped

1 clove garlic, minced

1 tsp. fresh ginger, diced

1/2 tsp. cumin

1/2 tsp. curry powder

1/4 tsp. cayenne pepper

1/2 can fire roasted tomatoes

1/2 cup dry red lentils

1 cup vegetable broth

1/2 cup water

1 tsp. brown sugar

1 tsp. salt

Heat olive oil in a medium sized saucepan and sautee yellow onion until caramelized. Add ginger, garlic, cumin, curry powder, cayenne pepper and sautee 30 seconds more.

2  Add tomatoes, lentils, broth, water, sugar, and salt and bring to a boil. Stir, reduce heat to simmer, and cover.

3  Cook until lentils are at desired texture. Add additional salt or sugar to taste.

4  Serve warm with rice.

# Vanilla oatmeal cookies

Serves 10

vegetarian

things you need

1 1/2 cups rolled oats

3/4 cup sugar

1 tsp. salt

2/3 cup vegetable oil

1 tsp. baking powder

1 egg

1/2 cup soy flour

1/2 tsp. vanilla extract

Preheat oven to 375F.

2  Combine oats, sugar, egg, and salt. Add baking powder and flour and stir well.

3  Drop by teaspoonful onto greased cookie sheet. Bake 7-8 minutes until brown on the edges.

4  Cool slightly before moving to a wire cooling rack.

# Carving apple heads

An artistic activity to occupy the time while you are staying awake the night of the equinox, observing the balance of darkness and light.

## things you need

Apples

Carving tools

Use whatever tools you have at hand to carve tiny heads and faces into your apples. These can be placed on your autumn altar or traded and eaten when you are done. If you can't be bothered to do all that  carving, you can at least cut the apple in slices across its core, revealing the pentagram in its center.

# Notes

# Notes

Cobweb by Marta Diarra (CC BY 2.0)

# Halloween/Samhain

Halloween and Samhain are the sister holidays to Walpurgisnacht and Beltane. These times of transition for the spirit world oppose each other and, where Walpurgisnacht was the last day for the darker spirits and Beltane the first day of the year for fairies, the spirits of light and darkness trade places again. It is time for celebrations of Indulgence and spectacle.

Pumpkin carving is not optional in our house. The seeds from carving pumpkins can be tasty when toasted and salted, but they make terrible pies. Be sure to use sugar pie pumpkins to get the desired flavor from your pumpkin. If you have any leftover cream cheese after making this pie recipe, it tastes great on those soft pretzels!

Twisted soft pretzels

Be bim bop

Cream cheese pumpkin pie

Horse's Neck

Ritual: Realistic wound makeup

# Twisted soft pretzels

Serves many

vegan

things you need

1 pkg. active dry yeast

1 Tbsp. sugar

1 1/4 cup warm water

4-5 cups flour

2 tsp. salt

4 tsp. baking soda

Poppy seeds

Coarse salt

Dissolve yeast in 1/4 cup water and 1 Tbsp. sugar. Stir in remaining 1 cup water.

Mix 4 cups flour and 2 tsp. salt in another bowl. Add the yeast mixture and combine with hands. If needed, add additional flour to make a stiff dough.

Knead ~10 minutes until smooth and elastic. Roll into a ball. Place in a greased bowl, turning twice to coat the top. Let rise in a warm place until doubled in size, about 45 minutes.

Divide dough into quarters, then divide each quarter into 4 balls of dough. Shape into pretzel shapes.

In a pot, dissolve 4 tsp. baking soda in 4 cups water and bring to a boil. One at a time, drop pretzels into boiling water for 1 minute. Remove and drain.

Place drained pretzels on buttered baking sheets. Sprinkle with salt and poppy seeds. Bake at 475F for about 10-12 minutes.

Cool on a rack and serve.

# Be bim bop

things you need

1 cup white basmati rice

2 beets

2 cups roasted squash, sliced

1 lemon

4 eggs

1/2 Tbsp. Sesame oil

1 Tbsp. Soy sauce

1 tsp. brown sugar

1/2 Tbsp. Rice vinegar

1 tsp. Finely minced ginger

Sesame seeds

Rinse rice in cold water. Pour off the cloudy water and repeat. Steam rice in a rice cooker according to instructions.

Meanwhile, cut acorn or butternut squash in half and bake in oven for about 30 minutes. Cool and slice.

Peel beet and cut into small matchsticks. Squeeze the juice of a lemon over the beets and toss to coat.

Prepare sauce by combining sesame oil, soy sauce, vinegar, ginger, and sugar.

After rice is cooked, divide into bowls. Top with beets, squash, and sesame seeds.

Fry eggs in sesame oil over easy to over medium. Season and place on top of rice bowls. Serve with sauce.

# Cream cheese pumpkin pie

Serves 6-8

vegetarian

## things you need

1 8 oz. pkg. cream cheese, softened

2 cups pumpkin puree made from 1 roasted sugar pumpkin

1 cup sugar

1/4 tsp. salt

1 egg + 2 yolks, slightly beaten

1 cup half and half

1/4 cup melted butter

1 tsp. vanilla extract

1/2 tsp. ground cinnamon

1/4 tsp. ground ginger

1 pie crust

Preheat oven to 350F. Place crust in a 9 inch pie pan and press down along the bottom and all sides and pinch and crimp the edges. Put the shell in the freezer for 1 hour.

2  Fit a piece of foil to cover the shell completely and fill with dry beans. Bake for 10 minutes until crust is set.

3  In a bowl, beat cream cheese, pumpkin, sugar, and salt until combined. Add eggs, half and half, and melted butter and beat until combined. Add vanilla, cinnamon, and ginger and mix until combined.

4  Pour filling into warm crust and bake 50 minutes or until center is set. Cool to room temperature.

# Horse's Neck

Serves 1

## things you need

2 oz. cognac

4 oz. ginger beer

Dash of Angostura bitters

Ice

Lemon zest

# Ritual: Realistic wound makeup

This technique is used for film and stage. There are so many options for types of wounds for your costume. Use black instead of red for scabs.

## things you need

Skin colored concealer
Red make up stick
Toilet paper
Karo syrup
Red food coloring
Liquid latex

Clean the area of skin you plan to use. Roll the tp into strips to outline a gash shape (elongated oval). Stick it down with liquid latex, smoothing and covering the tp and interior of the wound.

Paint the interior of the wound with red makeup then coat the toilet paper and edges of the wound with concealer. Repeat as needed until desired effect is achieved. Use the red Karo syrup as fake blood for the finishing touch.

# Notes

# Notes

# Winter Solstice

In the dark days of winter, the solstice brings a celebration of light. Candles, fairy lights, hearth fires, and sparkly decorations in the night bring us out of our homes for parties and a break from winter homebody syndrome. We make and bring gifts of food to our neighbors. Some of the craft projects that we began during the Autumn Equinox are completed and passed along as gifts.

Some of us stay awake during the longest night of the year, keeping watch. This is not a time to be wasteful because winter is only halfway over. Instead, humble acknowledgment and sharing of the supplies and resources we do have is how we prefer to acknowledge the season, with a dash of indulgence (usually in the form of sweet treats).

King crab with steamed artichokes

Wild rice pilaf with mushrooms and leek

Orange glazed carrots

Gingerbread cake with candied lemons

Ritual: Gifting—Chocolate dipped dried apricots

# King Crab with Steamed Artichokes

Serves 6

things you need

6 lbs. king crab legs, thawed

1 bottle white cooking wine

4 lemons, cut in half

1 full head garlic, split in thirds

3 artichokes

Melted butter for serving

Cut the top of the artichokes off and any excess stem beyond 1 inch. Rinse thoroughly.

In a large pot with a steamer, add a couple inches water, 1/3 of the head of garlic, smashed, and half a lemon, quartered.

Place steamer in pot and add artichokes. Bring to a boil, cover, and reduce to simmer for about 30 minutes, until the outer leaves can be pulled off easily.

Meanwhile, in a large stockpot, add wine, lemons, and remaining 2/3 head of garlic and bring to a boil.

Add crab legs to the stockpot and cover the pot. The crab legs will not be covered by the wine, but that is ok because we are steaming them. Cook for 5 minutes until cooked through.

Cover your dining table in paper grocery bags, melt some butter in the microwave in small bowls, and serve everything family style with crusty bread and lots of napkins.

# Mushroom, Leek, and Wild Rice Pilaf

Serves 4-6

vegan

## things you need

1 Tbs sesame oil

1 leek, cleaned, halved, and chopped

3 cups mixed fresh mushrooms, sliced

3 garlic cloves, sliced

1/4 tsp. dried thyme

1 1/2 cups wild rice

3 cups vegetable stock

1/4 cup cooking wine

1 Tbsp. soy sauce

1/4 cup chopped pecans

Preheat oven to 375F. Heat oil in a dutch oven over medium heat. Add leeks and cook until soft.

2 Add mushrooms and cook another 5-10 minutes until they start to brown. Add garlic and thyme and cook for 1 additional minute.

3 Add rice, wine, and soy sauce and simmer until almost all liquid is absorbed. Add broth and 1 cup water and return to a boil.

4 Place lid on dutch oven and bake for 45 minutes. Remove lid and cook for another 30 minutes or until most of the liquid is absorbed.

5 Remove from oven. Let stand for 5 minutes, then add nuts. Season to taste.

# Orange Glazed Carrots

Serves 4-6

vegan

things you need

2 cups carrots, cut into sticks

Zest and juice of 1 orange

1/2 cup orange juice

1 clove garlic, sliced

1/4 tsp. thyme

1/2 Tbsp. margarine

Salt and pepper

Slowly melt butter in a skillet with carrots, garlic, and thyme. When skillet is hot and you can begin to smell the garlic, add orange juice

Simmer and reduce over medium low heat until carrots are at desired texture. If you like your carrots soft, add 1 cup OJ. If you like them crisp, only add 1/2 cup OJ.

3 Season with salt and pepper. Remove from heat.

4 Add zest and fresh juice of one orange before serving.

# Gingerbread cake with candied lemons

Serves 9

vegetarian

things you need

1/2 cup butter

2 eggs

1/2 cup sugar

1 cup milk

1/4 cup molasses

1/4 tsp. salt

1 1/2 tsp. baking soda

1 tsp. cinnamon

1/4 tsp. nutmeg

2 tsp. ground ginger

2 cups rye flour

Zest of 1 lemon

2 lemons

1 cup sugar

Juice of one lemon

3/4 cup water

Cut lemons into 1/8 inch thick rounds. Discard ends and seeds.

Combine sugar, water, and lemon juice in a large pan. Heat and stir until sugar is dissolved. Add lemon slices in a single layer and simmer gently, turning occasionally, for about 15 minutes. Remove from heat.

Remove lemon slices from pan and place on waxed paper. Cool completely and set syrup aside.

Cream butter, sugar, and molasses in a mixing bowl. Beat in the eggs and add the remaining ingredients.

Pour the batter into a greased, floured, 9 inch square pan. Bake at 350F for about 25 minutes.

Remove from oven. Cool for 10 minutes in the pan, then remove from pan and cool
completely.

Arrange candied lemons on top of cake and drizzle with lemon syrup.

Alternatively, this cake is delicious served warm!

# Ritual: Gifting

Gifts of food are fitting for Winter Solstice. Here is our recipe for chocolate dipped apricots.

## things you need

2 cups Dried apricots (Blenheim variety is best)
1 cup semisweet baking chocolate
Sweetened coconut
Crushed nuts (any variety)

Spread coconut on a baking sheet and toast lightly in the oven. Meanwhile, melt chocolate in a double boiler. Dip apricots halfway into chocolate, then dip in toasted coconut or crushed nuts and leave some plain. Place dipped apricots on a cold baking sheet covered with a sheet of wax paper. Place the baking sheet in the freezer briefly until chocolate is set. Box them up with waxed paper.

# Notes

# Notes

Orange by Jin Choi (CC BY-SA 2.0)

Made in the USA
Las Vegas, NV
19 October 2021